Ulrich Renz / Barbara Brinkmann

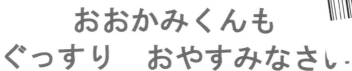

おおかみくんも
ぐっすり　おやすみなさい

Sleep Tight, Little Wolf

バイリンガルの絵本

翻訳:

Mari Freise-Sato (日本語)

Pete Savill (英語)

sefa

Download audiobook at:

www.sefa-bilingual.com/mp3

Password for free access:

日本語：mp3 not yet available

英語： LWEN1423

ティム、きょうは　もうねようね。　またあした、いっしょに さがそう
ね。　おやすみなさい。

„Good night, Tim! We'll continue searching tomorrow.
Now sleep tight!"

そとは　もう　くらく　なりました。

It is already dark outside.

でも ティムは なにを しているのでしょう?

What is Tim doing?

ティムは、こうえんに でかけていきます。

なにを さがしに いくのでしょう？

He is leaving for the playground.

What is he looking for there?

さがしていたのは、おおかみくんでした。
ティムは　おおかみくんが　いないと　ねむれません。

The little wolf!
He can't sleep without it.

あれ、こんどは　だれが　でてきたのでしょう？

Who's this coming?

でてきたのは　マリーです。

マリーも　ボールを　さがしにきたのです。

Marie!

She's looking for her ball.

こんどは　トビーが　でてきました。
なにを　さがしているのでしょう？

And what is Tobi looking for?

さがしていたのは、ショベルカーです。

His digger.

ナーラも　なにかを　さがしに　やってきました。
なにを　さがしているのでしょう？

And what is Nala looking for?

それは　おにんぎょうでした。

Her doll.

「みんな　おうちに　かえって、ねなくても　いいのかな。」
ねこさんは　とても　しんぱいに　なりました。

Don't the children have to go to bed?
The cat is rather surprised.

そして　また　やってきたのは. . .

Who's coming now?

ティムの　ママと　パパです。

ママと　パパも　ティムが　いないと　　ねむれません。

Tim's mum and dad!

They can't sleep without their Tim.

そして　もっと　たくさんの　ひとが　やってきました。

マリーの　パパと、トビーの　おじいさんと、ナーラの　ママです。

More of them are coming! Marie's dad.

Tobi's grandpa. And Nala's mum.

さあ、はやく　かえって　いそいで　ねよう！

Now hurry to bed everyone!

おやすみ、ティム。 あしたは もう さがさなくても いいんだよ。

„Good night, Tim!
Tomorrow we won't have to search any longer."

おおかみくんも　ぐっすり　おやすみなさい。

Sleep tight, little wolf!

More about me ...

Que duermas bien, pequeño lobo
Schlaf gut, kleiner Wolf

Ulrich Renz / Barbara Brinkmann

español · bilingüe · alemán

Schlaf gut, kleiner Wolf
راحت بخواب، گرگ کوچک

Ulrich Renz / Barbara Brinkmann

Deutsch · bilingual · Persisch (Farsi)

Dors bien, petit loup
Sleep Tight, Little Wolf

Ulrich Renz / Barbara Brinkmann

français · bilingue · anglais

نم جيدا أيها الذئب الصغير
Sov gott, lilla vargen

Ulrich Renz / Barbara Brinkmann

العربية · ثنائي اللغة · السويدية

Sofðu rótt, litli úlfur
Όνειρα γλυκά, μικρέ λύκε

Ulrich Renz / Barbara Brinkmann

Íslenska · tvímála · gríska

Dorme bem, lobinho
Suaviter dormi, lupe parve

Ulrich Renz / Barbara Brinkmann

português · bilingue · latino

Schlaf gut, kleiner Wolf
おおかみくんも
くっすり　おやすみなさい

Ulrich Renz / Barbara Brinkmann

Deutsch · bilingual · japanisch

잘 자, 꼬마 늑대야
Slaap lekker, kleine wolf

Ulrich Renz / Barbara Brinkmann

한국어 · 양국어 · 네덜란드어

Приятных снов, маленький волчёнок
Sleep Tight, Little Wolf

Ulrich Renz / Barbara Brinkmann

русский · двуязычный · английский

راحت بخواب، گرگ کوچک
Schlaf gut, kleiner Wolf

Ulrich Renz / Barbara Brinkmann

فارسی · دوزبانی · آلمانی

Que duermas bien, pequeño lobo
نم جيدأ أيها الذئبُ الصغير

Ulrich Renz / Barbara Brinkmann

español · bilingüe · árabe

സുഖമായി ഉറങ്ങൂ
ചെന്നായി കുഞ്ഞേ
Dormi bene, piccolo lupo

Ulrich Renz / Barbara Brinkmann

മലയാളം · ദ്വിഭാഷാ · ഇറ്റാലിയൻ

Dormi bene, piccolo lupo
जम के सोना, छोटे भेड़िये

Ulrich Renz / Barbara Brinkmann

italiano · bilinguale · hindi

ውብ ድቃስ፣ ጓኛኛዬ ተኩላ
Selamat tidur, si serigala

Ulrich Renz / Barbara Brinkmann

አማርኛ · ሁለት ቋንቋ · Malaysian

Śpij dobrze, mały wilku
ძილი ნებისა, პატარა მგელო

Ulrich Renz / Barbara Brinkmann

polski · Dwujęzyczna · gruziński

Солодких снів, маленький вовчику
잘 자, 꼬마 늑대야

Ulrich Renz / Barbara Brinkmann

українська · двомовний · корейська

Children's Books for the Global Village

Ever more children are born away from their parents' home countries, and are balancing between the languages of their mother, their father, their grandparents, and their peers. Our bilingual books are meant to help bridge the language divides that cross more and more families, neighborhoods and kindergartens in the globalized world.

Little Wolf also proposes:

The Wild Swans

Bilingual picture book
adapted from
a fairy tale by
Hans Christian Andersen

▶ Reading age 5 and up

www.childrens-books-bilingual.com

NEW! Little Wolf in Sign Language

Home	Authors	Little Wolf	About

Bilingual Children's Books - in any language you want

Welcome to Little Wolf's Language Wizard!

Just choose the two languages in which you want to read to your children:

Language 1:

[French ⌄]

Language 2:

[Icelandic ⌄]

[Go!]

Learn more about our bilingual books at www.childrens-books-bilingual.com. At the heart of this website you will find what we call our "Language Wizard". It contains more than 60 languages and any of their bilingual combinations: Just select, in a simple drop-down-menu, the two languages in which you'd like to read "Little Wolf" or "The Wild Swans" to your child — and the book is instantly made available, ready for order as an ebook download or as a printed edition.

As time goes by ...

... the little ones grow older, and start to read on their own. Here is Little Wolf's recommendation to them:

BO & FRIENDS

Smart detective stories for smart children

Reading age: 10 + - www.bo-and-friends.com

Wie die Zeit vergeht ...

Irgendwann sind aus den süßen Kleinen süße Große geworden

– die jetzt sogar selber lesen können. Der kleine Wolf empfiehlt:

MOTTE & CO

Kinderkrimis zum Mitdenken

Lesealter ab 10 – www.motte-und-co.de

About the authors

Ulrich Renz was born in Stuttgart, Germany, in 1960. After studying French literature in Paris he graduated from medical school in Lübeck and worked as head of a scientific publishing company. He is now a writer of non-fiction books as well as children's fiction books. – www.ulrichrenz.de

Barbara Brinkmann was born in Munich, Germany, in 1969. She grew up in the foothills of the Alps and studied architecture and medicine for a while in Munich. She now works as a freelance graphic artist, illustrator and writer. – www.bcbrinkmann.com

© 2018 by Sefa Verlag Kirsten Bödeker, Lübeck, Germany
www.sefa-verlag.de

sefa

IT: Paul Bödeker, München, Germany
Font: Noto Sans

ISBN: 9783739922782

Version: 20180225